INDONESIA

MALI

MEXICO

MONGOLIA

JAPAN

USA

NETHERLANDS

USA

SAUDI ARABIA

NORWAY

This Is My House

Best wishes to you and all in your home,

Arthur Dorros

Written and illustrated by
Arthur Dorros

SCHOLASTIC
HARDCOVER

SCHOLASTIC INC. / New York

To Phoebe

The houses pictured in this book are not the only types to be found in the respective countries. In any country, many types of housing can be found.

Library of Congress Cataloging-in-Publication Data
Dorros, Arthur.
This is my house / written and illustrated by Arthur Dorros.
p.   cm.
Summary: Text and illustrations depict the different types of houses lived in by children all over the world. On each page "This is my house" will appear in the appropriate native language.
ISBN 0-590-45302-5
1. Dwellings — Juvenile literature.   [1. Dwellings.]   I. Title.
NA7120.D65   1992
728—dc20   91-34273
                                                                                          CIP
                                                                                           AC

12   11   10   9   8   7   6   5   4   4   5   6   7/9
Printed in the U.S.A.   36
First Scholastic printing, September 1992
Design by Adrienne Syphrett

The illustrations in this book are watercolor and pencil paintings.

This Is My House

This is my house. My grandfather built it.
When we put on a new roof, the house
will keep us warm and dry again.

これは私の家です。

COH-ray WAH wah-TASH-ee-no EE YAY DESS

This is my house.

JAPAN

A house on wheels in Yugoslavia

A thatch house in Fiji

A tree house in the Solomon Islands

Mud Houses in Cameroon

People make houses out of whatever they can find. There are houses with walls of stone, or wood, or mud, or grass.

There are houses with walls of paper, walls of snow, even houses on wheels.

Stone houses in Israel

An igloo in Canada

Brick houses in China

Greetings from Seattle

A tent in Tibet

Thousands of years ago, huts could be made
of mammoth bones covered with animal hides
or branches covered with leaves.
Caves were also a place to be safe and warm.

Bu benim evimdir.
BOO BEH-nim EH-vim-deer
This is my house.

My family made our house in a cave. We carved the cave into a tall rock and put in windows. We painted the inside walls white.

It's different from the caves people lived in long ago.

TURKEY

USA

This is my house.
THIS IZ MY HOWS

This is where I live right now. My family is staying in our car. We will move into a house when we can.

SAUDI ARABIA

هـذا منزلي .

HAH-zah mon-ZILL-ee
This is my house.

I live in a tent in the desert. Tents
are movable houses. We need to move a lot
to find water and food for our animals.

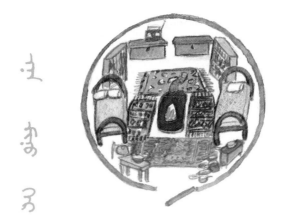

What's in a yurt

AY-neh MIH-nee GER
This is my house.

Our tent in the mountains has a door.
A floor and carpets keep us off the cold ground.
We can carry our tent, called a *yurt*, when
we move.

MONGOLIA

Esta casa é minha.

EHS-tah CAH-zah EH MEEN-yah

This is my house.

My whole house is made of plants. Where we live, there are plants all around us. We use dried plants called *thatch* to cover the roof.

Many families live together in our house.

BRAZIL

SAMOA

O lou fale lenei.
OH low-oo FALL-ay le-NAY
This is my house.

Our house is as round as a coconut.
Everyone in the family helped build our house.
We built it without walls so the air would blow in.
The breeze keeps the house cool during the hot days.

This is my house.
THIS IZ MOY HAYOWS

We use wood from the forests to make
strong houses and other buildings.
We cut up logs and nail the wood together.

NEW ZEALAND

RUSSIA

Это мой дом.
ETT-ah MOY DOME
This is my house.

We live in a wooden house made of logs.

NEW GUINEA

Dispela emi haus bilang mi.
dis-PEL-ah EM-mee HOWS BEE-long MEE
This is my house.

We live in a house on wooden stilts.

Dette er mitt hus.
DETT-teh AIR MITT HOOS
This is my house.

Our wooden house has a roof that grows.
It is covered with moss and other plants.

NORWAY

Akax utaxawa.
ah-KAH oo-tah-HAH-wah
This is my house.

I live in the high mountains, where there are few trees. We built our house out of stone.

BOLIVIA

EGYPT

هـذا منزلي .
HAH-zah mon-ZILL-ee
This is my house.

We need to add new thatch to the roof
of our stone house every year. The thatch
wears away, but the stone doesn't. A stone
building can last for thousands of years.

Esta es mi casa.
EHS-**tah** EHS MEE CAH-**sah**
This is my house.

Our house is made of mud. It is almost
finished. We form *adobe* bricks from wet mud.
Then the bricks are dried in the sunlight.
We fill cracks and smooth the walls with more mud.
    After our day's work, we visit my grandmother.
She built her adobe house by herself.

MEXICO

MALI

Ni ye n'ka sò ye.
NEE YAY nay-KAH SOY YAY
This is my house.

Each of these mud brick buildings is
a part of my house. My grandparents, parents,
brothers, and sisters have their own buildings.
The buildings are connected by a wall.
My grandfather carved pictures from stories
on the walls and doors of our house.

Ini rumah saya.
EEN-ee ROOM-ah SIGH-ah
This is my house.

In my house, the garden is part of the living room. Everyone in the family lives in rooms around the garden. Rain falls into the garden, but the rest of the house stays dry. The wall of dried mud that surrounds our house has its own roof, so the wall won't wash away.

INDONESIA

This is my house.
Each pueblo also has its own language.

Our houses connect together to form a *pueblo*.
Many families live close together in the pueblo.
My best friend lives at the top of that ladder.

PUEBLO, USA

Dit is mejn huis.
DIT ISS MINE HAOOS
This is my house.

We live in houses that are connected, too.
My father is a bricklayer. He uses baked mud bricks
to build rows and rows of houses.

NETHERLANDS

呢間係我間屋

This is my house.

The building I live in is made of cement and steel.
Families live in groups of rooms called *apartments*
on each floor.

Workers on bamboo scaffolding thirty floors high
are finishing another apartment building. People
from apartments below hang laundry on the scaffolding.

HONG KONG

HONG KONG
CONSTRUCTION

THAILAND

นี่คือบ้านฉัน.

NEE BEN BAHN CONE CHUN

This is my house.

My houseboat floats through the waves. We move our house around the city to sell fish we catch. At night our house rocks us to sleep.

Houses can be built into the sky, or on the water.

People without houses make shelters from cardboard or whatever they can find. A house can be a small room or a tall building.

People who live in the same part of the world can live in different kinds of houses.

And people who live in different parts of the world can live in the same kinds of houses.

A house can be big or small,
in the country or in a city.
Wherever it is, the people who live
in a house make it their home.

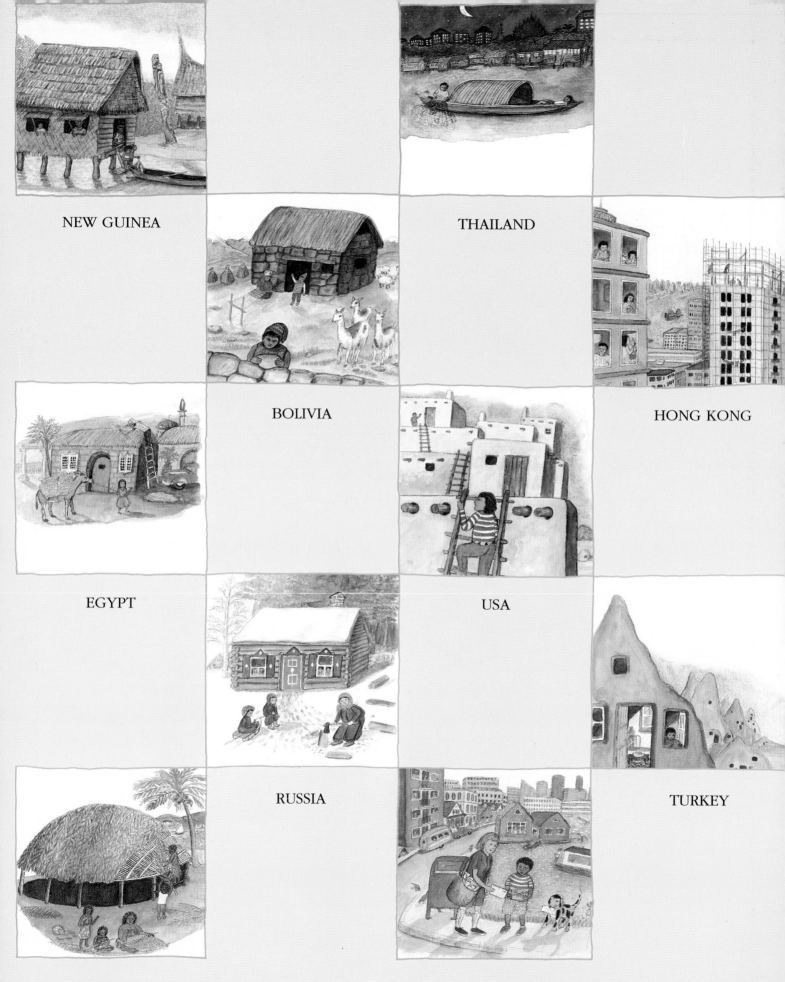

NEW GUINEA

THAILAND

BOLIVIA

HONG KONG

EGYPT

USA

RUSSIA

TURKEY

SAMOA

USA